Linking art to the world around us

artyfacts
Oceans

Contents

WRITTEN BY Janet Sacks and Polly Goodman

Deep blue sea

When we think of the seas or oceans we usually think of vast areas of blue-green water. The colour of the water in the sea depends on the light that shines on it. It also depends on how the light is reflected and absorbed by the water.

BLUE SEA

When light enters the sea, the water reflects some of it and absorbs some of it. Daylight is a mixture of many different colours of light, and these colours are reflected and absorbed in different amounts. Water hardly absorbs any blue-green light, but reflects it more than any other colour of light. This reflection of the blue-green light off the water is what makes the sea appear to be blue or green.

DEEP SEA

The deeper we go in the sea, the more light is absorbed. Below 1,000 metres, the waters of the oceans are almost completely dark. Here, animals have to produce their own light. They do this either by triggering chemical reactions in their body or by using light-making bacteria that live in their body.

SALTY WATER

Seawater is not pure water. It contains chemical elements found in rocks, which have dissolved over a long period. These are mostly chlorine, sodium, sulphur, magnesium, calcium and potassium. The main salt in the sea is sodium chloride, which is the same as ordinary table salt. The amount of salt in the sea can vary. In places where there is a lot of salt, the water is denser and the colour may be darker.

Linking und us

arty facts

Oceans

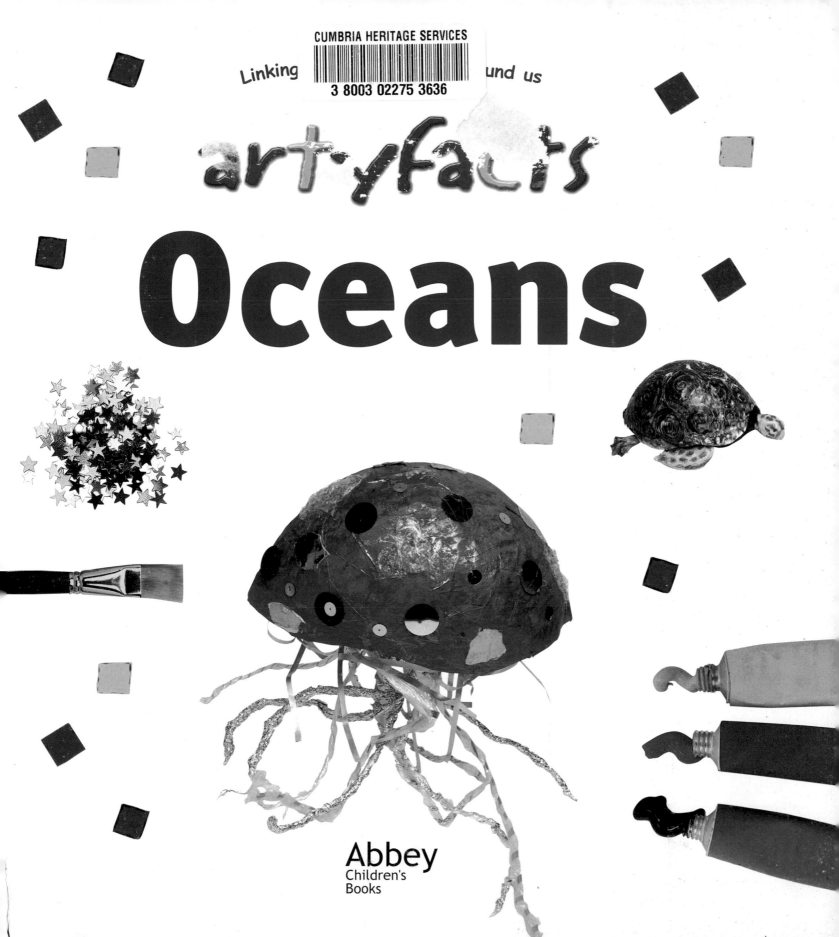

Abbey
Children's
Books

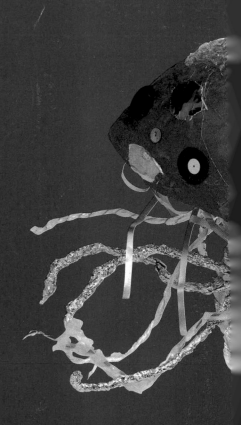

CONCEPT

Publisher: Felicia Law

Design: Tracy Carrington

Editorial Planning: Karen Foster

Research and Development: Gerry Bailey, Alec Edgington

PROJECT DEVELOPMENT

Project Director: Karen Foster

Editors: Claire Sipi, Hazel Songhurst, Samantha Sweeney

Design Director: Tracy Carrington

Design Manager: Flora Awolaja

Design and DTP: Claire Penny, Paul Montague,
James Thompson, Mark Dempsey

Photo and Art Editor: Andrea Sadler

Illustrator: Jan Smith

Model Artist: Sophie Dean

Further models: Sue Partington, Abigail Dean

Digital Workflow: Edward MacDermott

Production: Victoria Grimsell, Christina Brown

Scanning: Acumen Colour Ltd

Published by Abbey Children's Books
(a division of Abbey Home Media Group)

Abbey Home Media Group
435-437 Edgware Road
London W2 1TH
United Kingdom

Printed and bound by Dai Nippon, Hong Kong

Underwater picture

Fill your sea scene with shades of colour

Oceans

WHAT YOU NEED

paper and mount board

pencil

scissors

coloured pencils

tissue paper

glue

wire

1 With a pencil and paper, draw and shade in shapes of fish, shells, starfish, rocks and seaweed. Cut out the shapes.

2 Glue the shapes onto the backing card.

3 Tear pieces of tissue paper and paste them onto the card, overlapping the shapes to create different shades of colour.

4 Wrap tissue paper around a length of wire to make seaweed, and glue it onto your picture.

Overlap the shapes for a 3D effect

5

Seaweed power

You have probably seen seaweed washed ashore, lying on the sand or clinging to the pebbles on a beach. It is often smelly and looks quite disgusting. But seaweed is an essential part of ocean and shore life. It's a shelter or home for some sea creatures, and it's a highly nutritious food as well.

WHAT IS SEAWEED?

All seaweeds are simple plants called algae. They do not have proper roots, stems, leaves or flowers. Seaweed is full of nutrients, and is an important source of food for seashore creatures, such as mussels and crabs. It produces oxygen that all animals need to survive. Seaweeds can be green, brown, red or even purple. No seaweed grows deeper than 200 metres below the surface, as it needs sunlight to survive. Large seaweeds, such as kelp, have a root-like part that anchors them to rocks or to the sea bed. Smaller seaweeds, such as bladderwracks, have air-filled bubbles on their fronds that enable them to float.

KELP FORESTS

There are thousands of different species of seaweed. They range in size from the tip of a pencil to 100 metres long. Giant kelp grows faster than any other plant – up to 30 centimetres a day. With its hundreds of branches it looks like a scary sea creature, but it provides food and shelter for many underwater animals.

Seaweed collage

WHAT YOU NEED

paints and brush

paper

glue

encil

gold paint

sequins

aweed

mounting card

1 Draw an outline of several different seaweeds on paper. Paint and decorate with sequins.

2 Dry out the seaweed you have collected. Stick it over the top of your painting.

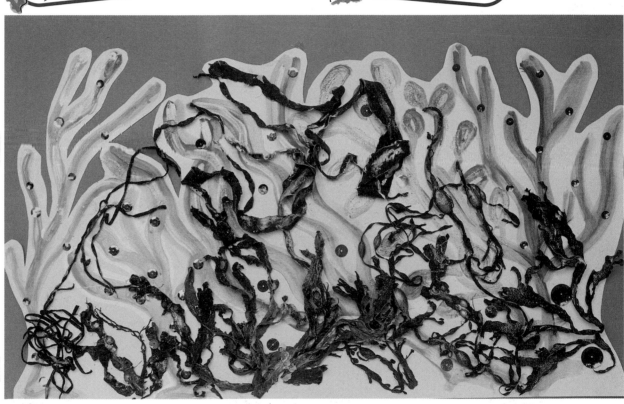

What other pictures can you make with your seaweed?

3 Cut around the seaweed outlines and mount the picture on card.

4 Add specks of gold paint onto your seaweed picture.

7

Jellyfish

Jellyfish drift in the ocean, trailing long tentacles beneath their umbrella-shaped bodies. These jelly-like bodies can be tinged red, brown, blue, yellow or mauve according to the colour of the water or what they eat. The fact that they are almost see-through helps camouflage them in the open ocean, where there is nowhere to hide.

WHAT ARE JELLYFISH?

Jellyfish have been around for over 650 million years – before dinosaurs roamed the Earth! They are not a type of fish – they belong to the invertebrate family, which means they do not have a backbone. Ninety-five per cent of a jellyfish's body is made up of water. A jellyfish does not have a heart, a brain or eyes – just a jelly-like body and tentacles to catch and stun food. The lion's mane jellyfish is the largest jellyfish, with a 2.4-metre body and tentacles longer than half a football pitch!

WATER ACROBATICS

Although jellyfish drift with the current, they can swim up and down by jet propulsion. Water is pushed out of the body, making the jellyfish move forwards.

A POWERFUL STING

Jellyfish use their sting to catch food and protect themselves. They can sense another creature's movements and this causes their stinging cells to shoot tiny tubes containing poison into the prey. The poison stuns or kills the prey.

A beautiful lagoon jellyfish.

Tickly tentacles

newspaper

glue

oon

ribbon

glitter

sequins

bubble wrap

paints and brush

thread

scissors

clear food wrap

1 Blow up a balloon. Rip pieces of newspaper up and glue over the top half of the balloon. When dry pop the balloon.

2 Paint and decorate the jellyfish body with glitter, sequins, foil and pieces of bubble wrap.

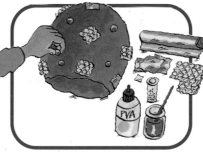

3 Twist lengths of clear food wrap and foil, and glue to the inside of the jellyfish's body.

Make a family of shimmering jellyfish with tentacles of different lengths and materials

4 Cut smaller lengths of ribbon and glue to the inside.

Attach a piece of thread from the centre of the body so you can hang your jellyfish from the ceiling.

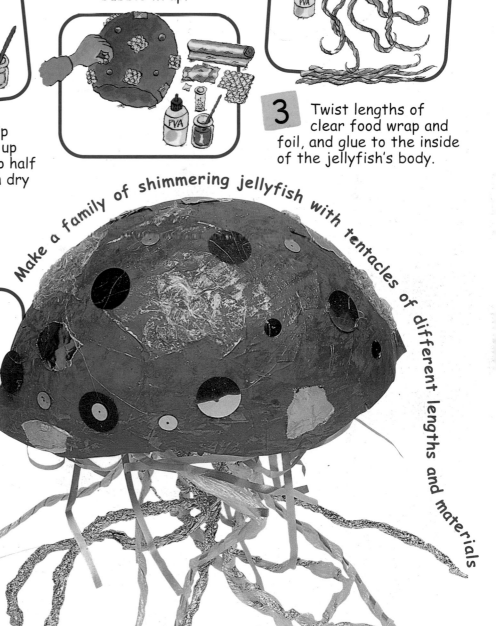

Claws and pincers

When you are on the beach, you may see a prawn paddling in a rock pool or a crab burying itself in the sand. These animals, along with lobsters, shrimps, krill, barnacles and crayfish, belong to the family of crustaceans. They are sea creatures that have a tough outer shell and many jointed legs.

CRABS

Hundreds of different crabs live on seashores in different parts of the world. They all have a shell, four pairs of legs, with which they walk sideways, and two claws for holding their prey. The hermit crab, however, doesn't have its own shell – it borrows someone else's instead!

A fiddler crab.

BIG AND SMALL

The biggest crab of all is the giant spider crab, whose outstretched claws can measure more than 4 metres from tip to tip – long enough to hug a hippopotamus! Spider crabs are an odd family – they like to dress up with bits of living sponge and seaweed and let these grow on them as a disguise. The smallest crab is the pea crab, which lives inside the shells of oysters and mussels. The male fiddler crab has one huge claw, which he uses to threaten other males and beckon a female. He feeds using his smaller claw.

PRAWNS AND SHRIMPS

Can you tell the difference between a shrimp and a prawn? A prawn has delicate claws on its front legs and a saw-like horn on its head, while a shrimp's front legs are broad and flat and it has no horn. Tropical prawns can grow as large as small lobsters. Some prawns and shrimps can change colour to match their surroundings.

LOBSTERS

Common lobsters come out of their rocky hiding places at night to look for food. Their two great claws crush, hold and tear their prey. But lobsters don't worry about losing one claw in a fight – it will grow again!

Clicking castanets

WHAT YOU NEED

paint and brush

elastic

foil

glue

sequins

shells

jar

scissors

sponge

1 Cover two jar lids with foil.

2 Ask an adult to help you make holes in one edge of each lid with the scissors. Thread through a piece of elastic and tie the ends together.

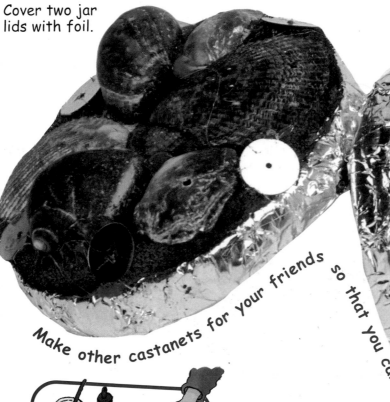

Make other castanets for your friends so that you can all click together!

3 Cut pieces of sponge, glue onto the tops of the lids, and paint.

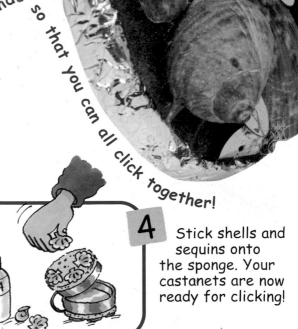

4 Stick shells and sequins onto the sponge. Your castanets are now ready for clicking!

11

Fishing nets

TRADITIONAL FISHING

People have fished in different ways for thousands of years without endangering fish supplies. Some people fish by throwing harpoons, others set traps, and many coastal communities fish from small boats not equipped for large catches

FREEZING THE CATCH

In the modern fishing industry, large refrigerator ships are able to stay out at sea for months, freezing the fish so that it doesn't go off.

ANIMALS IN DANGER

Nets are used to catch large number of fish. Drift nets, which can be up to 9 metres long, float behind fishing boats to catch any fish that swim at the surface, such as herrings, salmon and tuna. Unfortunately, other creatures, such as turtles, seals and sea birds, can get caught in th nets and die. Purse nets scoop up large shoals of tuna – and huge numbers of dolphin as well. An international ban on these nets is now in place to stop dolphins being endangered in this way. When trawlers trawl the sea bed for soles and rays, they also kill huge numbers of worms and shellfish that the fish feed on. It is very difficult to control the numbers of fish being caught, but every year, countries agree on the maximum number of fish that they will catch. This helps the situation, but overfishing is still a problem.

People all over the world eat fish. Each year many tonnes of fish are caught in the oceans, with sardines, Atlantic cod and mackerel being the main fish caught. However, we are overfishing. The fish being caught now are younger and smaller. This is a sign that we are not breeding enough fish to replace those that have been killed.

Oceans

Hook-a-fish game

1 Draw and cut out a large card circle for the pond base.

2 Cut a wide length of card to fit around the base circle. Glue the ends together and stick it to the base.

3 Paint and decorate your pond with coloured tissue paper and silver foil.

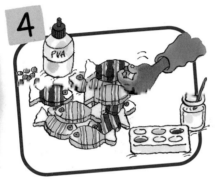

Cut out fish shapes from the polystyrene. Paint them and stick on sequins for eyes.

Play a game to see who can hook the fish the fastest!

5 Make small circles out of the wire as shown above. Attach these to the fishes' mouths.

6 To make the fishing rods, twist wire into hook shapes, then tie a length of string to a straw and attach a hook to the end of the string.

13

Sea cows

A manatee feeding its you[ng]

Sea cows graze on sea grass, which is how they got their name. They are really dugongs and manatees, large grey mammals that live in the sea. Although they are sea creatures, they breathe air and give birth to live babies, which feed on milk.

HOME OF THE SEA COW

Dugongs and mantees look very similar, and have only very slight physical differences. They are also found in different parts of the world: West Indian and West African manatees live in the tropical waters of the Atlantic. Freshwater Amazonian manatees are smaller, and live in South America in the Amazonian River. Duganons are found in the Arabian Gulf, on Africa's east coast, in the Pacific Ocean, and in largest numbers off northern Australia. The dugong has a dolphin-like tail and more rounded flippers than the manatee, which ha[s] a paddle-shaped tail.

LIFE UNDER WATER

Sea cows grow to roughly 3 metres long and weigh around 500 kilograms. They live in warm, shallow waters and as they graze, they leave behind trails of bare sand and uprooted sea grass. They can sta[y] underwater for 20 minutes, coming to the surface to breathe. They live for about 50 years.

MERMAIDS

Years ago, a great many sailors, as well as people walking along seashores, believed that they had seen mermaids out at sea. In fact, it is most likely that they had seen a manatee or dugong.

Magical mermaid

1

Soften clay and make a mermaid's head and body with it. When dry, paint.

2 Draw the two sides of a mermaid's tail on material and cut out. Glue the sides together, leaving a gap at the top. Cut sequins into pieces, and glue onto the tail.

3

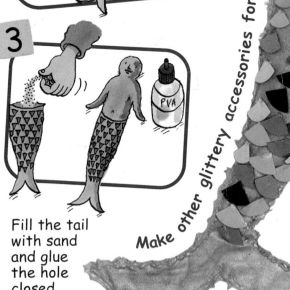

Make other glittery accessories for your mermaid

Fill the tail with sand and glue the hole closed. Then glue the body to the top of the tail.

4

Glue a shell bikini top onto the mermaid's body. Stick seaweed on her head for hair.

Draw and cut out a comb and mirror from card. Decorate with sequins and glitter.

5

15

Ice fields

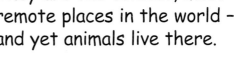

The North Pole is surrounded by the frozen Arctic Ocean, and the South Pole by the icy continent of Antarctica. They are the coldest, most remote places in the world – and yet animals live there.

POLAR BEARS

Polar bears live in the Arctic. Their thick white coats keep them warm and make them difficult to see in the white landscape. When hunting – usually for seals – a polar bear wanders alone over the vast floating ice sheets, called ices floe looking for holes where seals come up for air. Here it will wait patiently until a seal appears. Then, with one blow of the bear's huge paw and a bite at the back of the head, the seal is killed.

SEALS

Seals are found at both poles. Some species spend the winter under the ice sheet, and can stay underwater for up to 70 minutes before coming up for air. They go onto land to breed and give birth. The pups are covered in white woolly fur, which they shed after about a month.

PENGUINS

In the Antarctic, millions of penguins gather together in the summer to breed. Emperor penguins, however, breed at the start of winter. The male incubates the egg, keeping it off the ice, on his feet. This means he cannot feed, and by the time the chick hatches, he has lost half his body weight. Penguins are not like most birds because they cannot fly. Their wings are really flippers, more suited to swimming. They move better in the water than on land, swimming and diving so well that they have sometimes been mistaken for dolphins.

Emperor penguins on the Antarctic ice.

Penguin family

card

scissors

pencil

glue

foil

paints and brush

glitter

1 Draw 3 different size penguins on card. Paint them, and cut out.

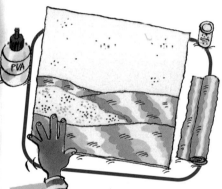

2 Decorate a sheet of card with paint, glitter and foil to make an icy background.

Create a chilly polar scene with stand-up penguin models!

3 Draw and cut out the shapes shown, and stick onto the backs of the penguins to make them stand.

4 Stand the penguins up in front of the icy background.

Rock pools

If you take a stroll along a seashore you are bound to find a rock pool. A unique variety of animals and plants, from starfish to seaweeds, make their homes in them. In these tiny sea worlds, plants and animals live together in a community where they help each other to survive.

HIGH AND LOW TIDES

Rock pools are transformed twice a day by the rise and fall of the tides. They fill up with salty seawater when the tide comes in, and then empty again when it goes out. And they are also hit by large, crushing waves and brisk ocean winds. Seashore plants and animals have learned to adapt to life in an environment that changes all the time.

DIFFERENT KINDS OF POOLS

Rock pools can be small, shallow puddles high up on the shore, or large, deep holes close to the sea. When the tides come in, the seawater brings with it fresh oxygen and food for the rock pool inhabitants.

ROCK POOL NEIGHBOURS

All kinds of creatures live together in a rock pool. Velvet swimming crabs scurry about the rocks, the common starfish moves through the water in search of food, molluscs such as winkles, whelks and limpets move slowly on their large fleshy 'feet'. Tiny fish called blennies dart behind the water plants. Seaweeds are essential to life in a rock pool. They provide oxygen and shelter from the sun, and protect animals such as shrimps, crabs and fish from predators. Animals such as slugs and snails also feed on these nutritious sea plants.

A red starfish

Oceans

3D seaside picture

shoebox lid

shells and pebbles

feathers

cardboard

glitter

ruler

pencil

clay

sand

scissors

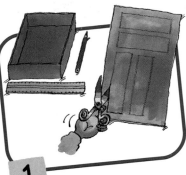

1 Make 2 card rectangles to fit longways inside the box lid. Make 2 rectangles that fit widthways.

2 Cut slits in the 2 shorter pieces and slot all 4 pieces together. Place inside the lid.

3 Paint the lid and sections. Glue shells all around the outside.

4 Glue glitter and sand inside the sections.

5 Fill the spaces with shells, feathers and pebbles, and glue them in.

Make starfish shapes from clay. When dry, paint and place in your treasure box

19

Oily feathers

The sea is a living world. Beneath the waves there is an enormous variety of life, from sea plants and tiny plankton to huge whales and sharks. But today, people are creating pollution, which is killing life in the oceans and poisoning the fish that people rely on for food.

OIL SPILLAGES

The worst polluter of all is oil. When oil tankers clean out their tanks, they leave oil slicks on the surface of the sea, which poison fish and coat the feathers of sea birds. When oil clogs an animal's fur or a bird's feathers, they can no longer swim or fly. They cannot keep warm and either die from cold, or poisoning caused by swallowing oil while trying to clean themselves. Animal rescue teams help by cleaning the birds and animals.

PEOPLE POLLUTE

Half of the world's population lives on or near the coast. Lots more people visit the coast for a beach holiday. All this means a greater amount of rubbish going into the sea. Litter kills – plastic packaging can strangle or suffocate animals, and glass and metal can cut them. Farms and factories also produce chemicals which are washed into the sea.

CONTROLLING POLLUTION

Countries have to agree on laws to stop dumping waste at sea, and to ban farms and factories from using pollutants. People can help too, by recycling rubbish and not leaving litter on beaches.

A seabird covered in oil.

Cormorant mobile

1 On card, draw the outline of a comorant's body and two huge wings. Cut them out.

2 Cover the inner side of the wings with silver foil.

3 Colour the rest of your cormorant with dark brown and black pastels and paints.

4 Make a fold along the inside edge of each wing and glue the wings onto the body of the cormorant.

Make other bird mobiles to fly in the breeze with your cormorant

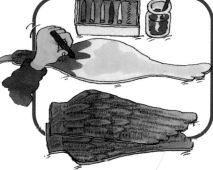

5 Attach a piece of gold thread from the top of the body, and a piece of elastic from each wing. Knot the thread and elastic together as shown.

Push the wings gently, and see how they move up and down.

21

Sea salt

Salt has always been important to us – we need it to stay healthy and replace the salt we lose from our bodies when we sweat. Most of the salt we use is mined as rock salt. But there are many people who take their salt from the sea.

SALT PANS

The sea contains a large amount of salt. In dry, hot countries, such as India or Africa, shallow pools, called pans, are built on the seashore. Sea water is pumped into these pans, then left to dry out, leaving the powdery salt behind.

THE DEAD SEA

The saltiest water in the world is in the Dead Sea It is called 'dead' because no fish except brine shrimps and very few plants can live in it. It is a huge lake, about 80 kilometres long, and its shore is the lowest place on the surface of the Earth, at about 399 metres below sea level.

FLAMINGOES IN FLORIDA

Flamingoes are birds that can stand high levels of salt. During the hurricane season, the shores of Florida flood. As the water evaporates, it turns salty and the brine shrimp hatch out. Flamingoes, feed the shrimp to their hungry fledglings.

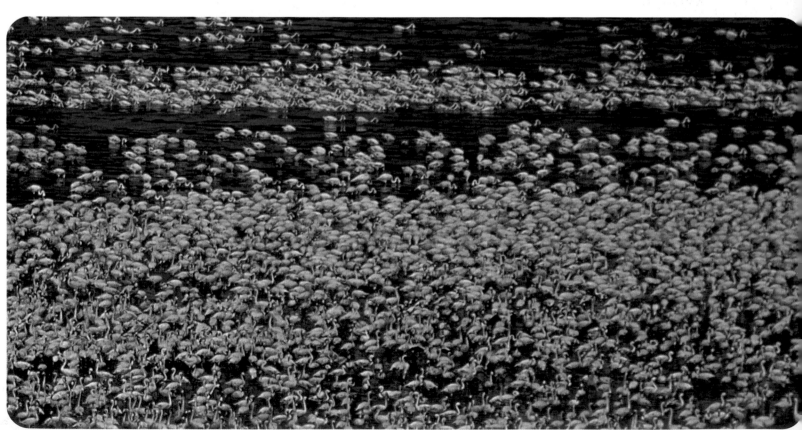

Salt dough flamingo

bowl

glitter

oil

salt

our

ater

paints and brush

wooden spoon

2 Flatten some of the dough into a circle. Make a landscape and flamingo with the rest, and put them on top.

1 Mix salt, oil, flour and water together in a bowl until you have a doughy mixture. Place the dough in a fridge for a few hours.

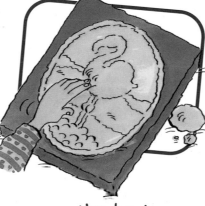

3 Bake at gas mark 5 (190°C) for 30 minutes. When cool, paint and decorate with glitter. Remember, you should not eat this!

You could add more feeding flamingoes to the background, or a stunning pink sunset sky

For instant colour, add a few drops of food colouring to the dough mixture.

Turtle tale

Thousands of years ago, turtles left the land to live in the sea. Over time, the turtles adapted to life in the salty ocean, developing flippers instead of legs, and crying salty tears to get rid of the salt they absorbed from the sea. But they must still come to the surface for air, and the females come ashore to lay their eggs.

LAYING EGGS

After mating in the sea, female turtles go ashore at night. They always return to the exact beach where they themselves hatched – and they may travel thousands of kilometres across oceans to the beach. There, the female digs a deep hole, and lays a clutch of up to 200 eggs, each about the size of a table tennis ball. Then she covers them with sand and returns to the sea. Although a female may only breed once every three years, she may come ashore several times to lay her eggs in one season.

UP AND AWAY

The eggs stay buried for several weeks. Eventually the babies hatch and start to dig their way out. They come out at night when there are fewer predators about – but how do they know when it is night? If the sand near the surface is hot, it is daytime, but when it's cool they know it is night-time and they make their way out and head straight for the sea.

A DIFFICULT JOURNEY

As the little turtles head for the sea, seabirds, crabs, iguanas, even foxes are lying in wait for a tasty meal. And many of those that survive their dangerous journey will reach the sea only to be eaten by fish. Even when they grow up, turtles are threatened. Their main enemy is people, who hunt turtles for their shells and meat.

The loggerhead turtle was given its name because of its large chunky head.

Loggerhead turtle

WHAT YOU NEED

balloon

newspaper

glue

scissors

tights

clay

paints and brush

1  Blow up the balloon and paste strips of newspaper all over with watered-down glue. Put on several layers and leave to dry. Then burst the balloon.

2 Mix paint with glue and cover the newspaper 'shell' with swirly circles. Leave to dry.

3 Soften the clay and make the head, feet and flippers of your turtle. Leave to dry and then paint them.

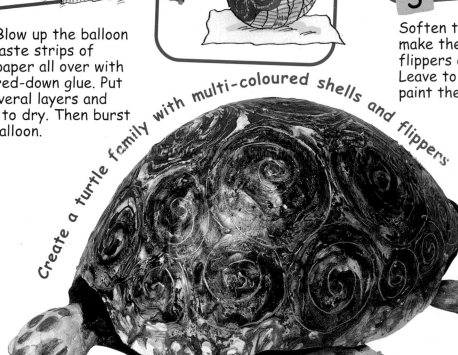

Create a turtle family with multi-coloured shells and flippers.

4 Cut around the shell, as shown.

5 Fill the tights with newspaper and use to stuff the shell.

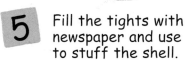

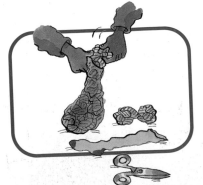

6 Make holes in the tights and glue in the head, feet and flippers.

On stilts

On tropical coasts, where forests come down to the water's edge, you will find tall trees known as mangroves standing on a thick tangle of roots. Here the tide washes in and out and the plants have adapted to living in salty water.

SURVIVING SALT

Most trees can't grow in waterlogged ground because the soil is too soft to support them and it lacks the oxygen that tree roots need. Yet trees in the mangroves live in thick mud, starved of oxygen, with their roots pickled in salt water. How do they survive? They have developed two special types of root. Stilt roots arch out from the trunk to support the tree, and breathing roots push up above the mud to take in oxygen. The trees are also able to get rid of salt through salt glands in their leaves.

LIFE IN THE MANGROVES

The mangroves are alive with creatures. Mangrove tree crabs live in the branches of the trees, only dropping into the water to escape danger. The mangrove cuckoo feeds on swamp insects, while several types of sea-snail munch mangrove leaves. But perhaps the most fascinating creature of all is the mudskipper – a fish that can breathe in both water and air. It has strong fins that help it skip across the mud. The Malayan mudskipper even has fins that form suckers so that it can climb trees!

Mangrove trees rising from the swamp.

Mangrove roots

Make a roots and branches picture of mangrove trees

1 On card, draw 2 mangrove trees with their branches above sea level and their roots below, as shown. Add a forest background.

Paint and decorate with glitter and coloured pencils. **2**

3 Cover the watery half of your picture with clear acetate.

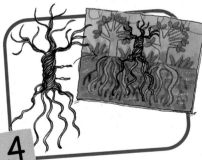

4 Use wire to make a third, weirdly-shaped tree. Twist strands of wire together to form the trunk, branches and roots. Fix to the centre of your picture by pushing through wire strands from the trunk and fastening behind.

5 Cut leaves from tissue paper and gold paper and stick to the wire frame. Mount your picture.

27

Desert islands

The ocean floor has all the features we see on land – mountains, valleys, volcanoes – but they lie in the depths of the sea, mostly hidden from view. Sometimes the peaks of these underwater mountains, or volcanoes, poke up through the waves. They form small islands, either on their own or in groups or chains. Islands are sprinkled throughout the world's oceans.

THE GALAPAGOS ISLANDS

All islands are separated, or isolated, from the mainland. Rare species of plants and animals are often found on islands where they are safe from the mainland predators. The Galapagos Islands in the Pacific Ocean, are named after the giant tortoises that live there – 'galapagos' means 'tortoise'. They can live for up to 200 years, and the males can

A marine iguana from the Galapagos Islands.

weigh up to 250 kilograms. Other rare creatures include the marine iguana – the only lizard to live and feed in the sea – and the flightless cormorant.

PIRATES

Islands have always been good hiding places for pirates because they can ambush, or make a surprise attack on, passing ships. In the 17th and 18th centuries, pirates known as buccaneers prowled along the coasts of America. They were waiting to attack the great Spanish galleons loaded with treasure, that were sailing home to Spain across the Atlantic Ocean. In the 18th century, when Dutch and British ships traded with China and Japan, they had to pass through the Straits of Malacca, between Malaysia and Sumatra. Here, pirates would lie in wait on the islands and attack passing ships in small boats. Piracy is still a danger there, even today.

CORAL ISLANDS

Coral islands, like the Maldives, lie in the warm waters of the Indian and Pacific Oceans. They form when soil and vegetation settle on coral atolls. A coral atoll is a ring of coral that has built up on a sunken mudbank or on the rim of the crater of a sunken volcano. Seeds brought by the wind or sea, such as coconuts, have planted themselves on the shores.

Oceans

WHAT YOU NEED

paper

pencil

aint and brush

black pen

teabag

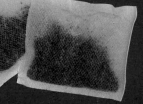

water

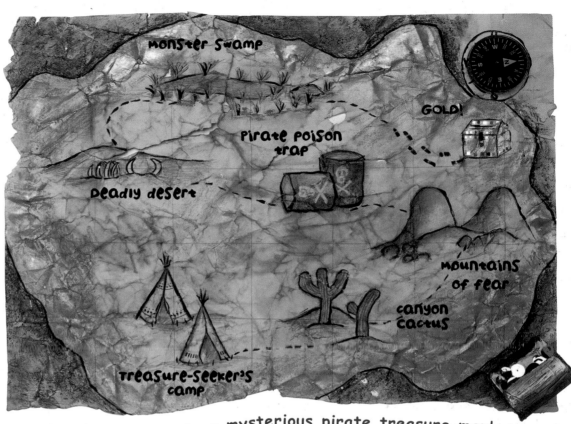

monster swamp

GOLD!

pirate poison trap

Deadly desert

mountains of fear

canyon cactus

treasure-seeker's camp

Make and decorate a mysterious pirate treasure map!

1 Draw the outline of an island on paper.

2 Mix a teabag with water and paint over your picture to make it look old. Leave to dry.

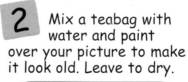

3 Draw on a compass and a treasure chest. Add dangerous obstacles on the way to the treasure.

4 Paint in all the details on your map, and the sea around the island.

5 Label the obstacles and make small tears around the map edges.

29

Deep-sea fish

Many strange and wonderful fish live in the deepest part of the ocean. This area is called the 'bathypelagic zone'. It stretches from 1 to 6 kilometres below the water's surface. From 3 kilometres down there is almost no light.

BIOLUMINESCENCE

The hatchet fish and the black devil deep-sea angler are two fish that can make their own light. This is called bioluminescence. It happens because a chemical in their body changes the energy stored in the fish's cells into light. The fish uses this light to search for food or to attract prey.

USEFUL EYES

The eyes of some deep-sea fish are fixed on short stalks sticking out from their head. The eyes can be turned so that the fish can look up, as well as to the front and side.

STRANGE SHAPES

Some deep-sea fish are strange shapes. The common gulper eel looks like a long tail with a mouth attached. The tripod or spider fish, looks like a three-legged stool! It has three long fins which it uses to sit on on the ocean floor. The Pacific fangtooth has a huge mouth with rows of long, curved, needle-sharp teeth.

Fishy monster

WHAT YOU NEED

coloured paper

pencil

old sock

glue

bottle tops

scissors

newspaper

sand

paints

paint-brush

1 Stuff the sock with scrunched-up strips of newspaper. Glue or tie the end closed.

2 Make the upper fin. Fold a piece of paper the length of your fish, mark out a zig-zag shape, and cut it out.

3 Glue the fin to the fish.

Make a weird creature from the deep!

4 To make the tail and side fins, fold the coloured paper like a fan and cut it into 3 pieces, 1 big and 2 small. Glue on the big piece for the tail fin and the small pieces for the side fins.

5 Mix the sand, glue and paint together and brush the mixture over the fish shape. Leave to dry. Stick on the bottle tops for the eyes.

High tide, low tide

Exploring the beach is fun, but be careful – the sea can catch you out! Water may rush up the beach and cut you off from the upper shore. The sea will rise, and it will be another six hours before it starts to sink. This is called high tide. When the sea goes out, it is called low tide.

THE PULL OF GRAVITY

When the Earth spins, the force called gravity stops everything from flying off it. Gravity pulls the Moon towards the Earth. But the Moon has its own gravity, which is strong enough to pull on the sea nearest to it, as it goes round the Earth. This pull causes tides, which in most parts of the world change every six hours.

SPRING AND NEAP TIDES

The Sun also has a pulling effect on the sea. Twice a month both the Sun and the Moon pull together, causing very high and very low tides known as spring tides. Twice a month the pull of the Sun and Moon is not strong, causing smaller tides called neap tides. The highest tide in the world takes place in the Bay of Fundy, Canada, where it can rise 16 metres – as high as a four-storey building.

WAVES AND CURRENTS

When the wind blows on the surface of the sea, it makes waves. But winds can also cause currents. These are like rivers of cold and warm water that travel around the oceans. Currents on the surface of the sea, like Florida's Gulf Stream, are driven by the wind. Deep ocean currents come from the cold polar regions and flow beneath the warmer water.

Shimmering moon

WHAT YOU NEED

- ~~ck~~ ~~white~~ ~~rd~~
- scissors
- glitter
- foil
- pencil
- glue
- sequins
- ~~aints~~ ~~brush~~
- polystyrene cup

1 Draw a large circle on card and cut it out.

2 Paint and decorate with glitter and sequins.

... Add a sprinkling of glitter around the edge

... Glue this magical moon to your bedroom window

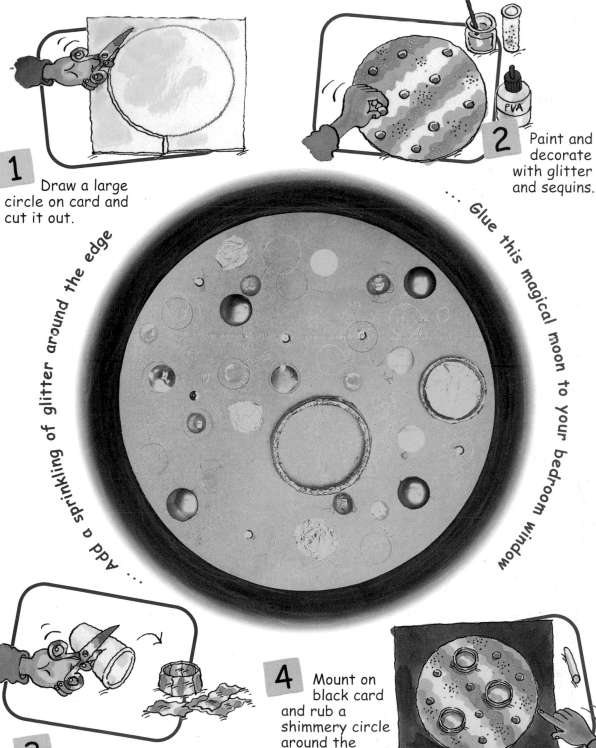

3 Cut rings out from the cup and cover in foil. Stick onto your moon to make craters.

4 Mount on black card and rub a shimmery circle around the moon with the white chalk.

Legs and suckers

What sea creature can change colour, has eight legs with suckers on them, can squirt out a black fluid called ink, has eyes similar to a human's and is considered to be the most intelligent of the invertebrates? Answer – the octopus!

SUCKERS

An octopus may have up to 240 suckers on its e[...] tentacles, or legs – once an octopus has attache[...] itself to something, there is no way that anyone [...] move it! If it loses a leg, another grows back.

LIVING ALONE

There are about 200 different types of octopus. They are found inside cave[...] in shallow seas near the shore. Octopuses live alone.

A BRAINY CREATURE

The octopus is considered the m[...] intelligent of the invertebrates [...] Experiments show that an octo[...] is able to learn that by removin[...] the lid from a jar, it can get to [...] food inside. An octopus's eyes a[...] more like a human's than an invertebrate's because they [...] able to see images.

DEFENDING ITSELF

As an octopus doesn't have [...] shell, how can it protect itse[...] against predators? In fact, the octopus is a master of disguise. It is able to change colour to match its surroundin[...] If this doesn't work, an octopus will release a cloud of black ink that temporarily blinds its enemy and destroys its sense of smell.

An octopus swimming in the sea.

Oceans

WHAT YOU NEED

sequins

ard

pencil

tissue paper

glue

foil

paints and brush

glitter

egg box

scissors

d

ghts

1 Draw an octopus head on card, cut out and paint.

2 Cut out segments from the eggbox and paint.

3 Glue the eggbox segments onto the octopus's body and decorate them with sequins.

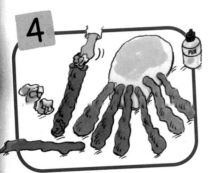

4 Stuff the tights with scrunched-up tissue paper and glue to the back of the octopus to make eight tentacles.

5 Stick blue tissue paper on a sheet of card. Glue on scrunched-up tissue paper rocks.

Glue the octopus in place. Make eyes from foil and sequins. Glue sequins on the tentacles.

Cut out and paint fish and starfish shapes. Glue th em to your picture, and decorate with glitter

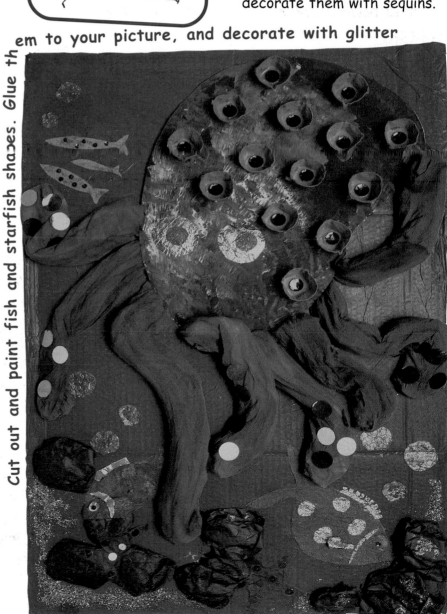

35

Ocean giants

Most whales are enormous creatures, but they move gracefully through their watery world, swimming, diving, rolling and leaping. They come up to the surface and breathe out in a great spray – and immediately take in more air. Then, with an upward thrust of their large tail fins, they dive back down into the deep waters in search of food.

WHAT IS A WHALE?

A whale is not a fish. It is a mammal like us, which means it is warm-blooded and gives birth to babies which are suckled with milk. Also like us, a whale breathes air, but its nostrils, called blowholes, are on the top of its head!

OCEAN GIANTS

The blue whale (above) is the biggest animal that has ever existed. At 150 tonnes, it's as heavy as about 25 elephants and can grow to over 30 metres long. And it has the biggest babies in the world, weighing 1,000 times more than a human baby at birth! It feeds on krill, which are tiny shrimp-like creatures swallowing hundreds in one gulp.

WHALES IN DANGER

Over the centuries whales have been hunted for their oil, blubber, meat and baleen – a comb-like plate in some whales' mouths that they use to filter food from the water. The number of whales in the oceans has been greatly reduced by hunting, and some species of whale have almost died out. There is now a worldwide ban on killing whales for money.

Papier-mâché whale

2 Cut out a tail shape from card and glue to the open end of the model.

3 Paint the whale.

1 Blow up the balloon and paste several layers of torn strips of newspaper onto it. Cover the whole balloon. When the newspaper is dry, pop the balloon.

Get your friends to see what treasures they can find inside the whale

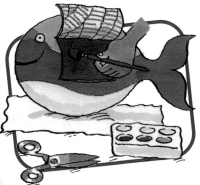

5 Glue in lengths of twisted food wrap and tissue paper.

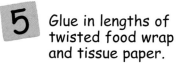

4 Cut a door in the side of the whale and paint inside.

6 On card, draw and paint a fish, an old boot, a tin can, seaweed, and so on. Cut them out, and put them inside your whale.

37

Jewels of

the sea

SHIMMERING CASES

There are several thousand different kinds of diatom in all different shapes and sizes. Some join together in patterns, and others float on their own like minute, glistening gems. Diatoms look like blobs of jelly inside a hard glassy shell. This shell, or case, is made out of silica. Some diatoms contain tiny drops of oil that help them to float in water. When a diatom dies, its silica case drops down onto the ocean floor.

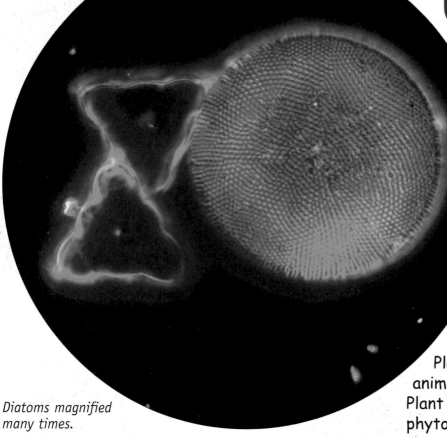

*Diatoms magnified
many times.*

SEA FOOD

Plankton is not just made up of plants. Tiny animals, called zooplankton, are also part of it. Plant plankton, including diatoms, is called phytoplankton. Phytoplankton is the first part of the ocean food chain, providing food for the zooplankton, which is then eaten by small fish. Larger fish then eat the small fish.

The top layer of the ocean is warmer than the waters below it. It receives plenty of sunlight and is the perfect place for microscopic plants, called plankton, to grow. These plants use sunlight to make their own food, in a process called photosynthesis. Diatoms are a type of plankton. They can be found in every ocean, just below the surface. There can be hundreds of diatoms in a drop of water.

SKELETON POWER

Toothpaste and scouring powder contain the remains of tiny fossilised diatoms. Over millions of years, the silica skeletons have been pressed down until the bottom layer becomes fossilised, or turned to stone. The strength of this material makes it suitable to use for grinding, sanding, smoothing or polishing.

Diatom art

1 Draw the outlines of different diatoms on card.

Choose jazzy colours for a vibrant look!

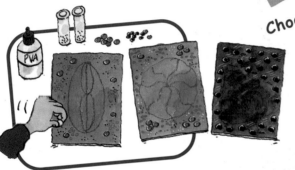

2 Paint and decorate the cards with sequins, glitter and clear food wrap.

3 Highlight the diatom outlines with paints, ribbon, pipe cleaners and black pen.

4 Mount your diatom pictures on coloured card.

Seahorses

The seahorse is a small fish, although it doesn't look like one. Its head looks like that of a tiny horse, and that is where it gets its name. It has a body made up of bony plates, a long snout and cylindrical-shaped mouth, and a long flexible tail to grasp on to sea plants. There are 35 different types of seahorse, from the tiny dwarf seahorse, which is only 2.5 centimetres long, to one that is 30 centimetres long.

LIFESTYLE

Seahorses are found in warm seas, near the shoreline, hidden among the seaweed and clinging to it with their tails. Because they are not very fast swimmers, they have to rely on camouflage to keep safe – there are plenty of crabs, tuna and rays around to prey on them. Some seahorses can change colour to match their background. Others grow leafy fronds to make them look like seaweed. As a result, seahorses are hard to spot.

SUPERDADS

Seahorses have the same partner throughout their lives – but it is the male seahorse that gives birth to the babies. Male and female seahorses do a lovely mating dance, twirling and raising their heads and – in some cases – turning fluorescent colours! Then the female seahorse lays hundreds of eggs into a special pouch that the male seahorse has on his front. The male is pregnant for nearly three weeks. The young are fed, given oxygen and kept safe in his pouch. Unfortunately, when they are born, there are many dangers waiting for baby seahorses. Storms tear them from their safe haven, leaving them to starve, and only an average of two of the hundreds that are born will reach adulthood.

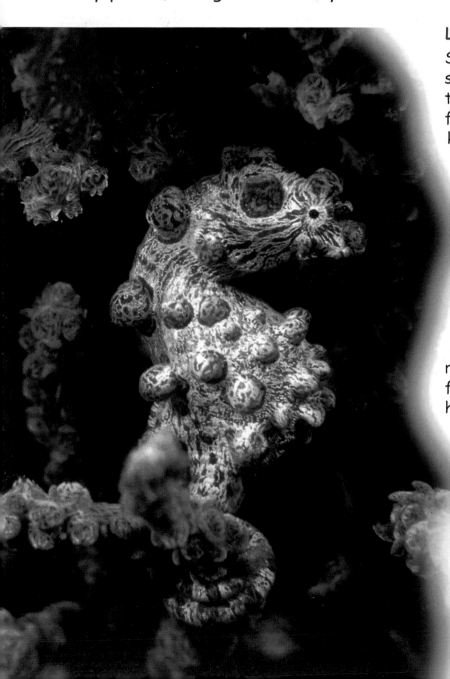

A colourful pygmy seahorse.

Watery grotto

WHAT YOU NEED

- paints and brush
- coloured paper
- card
- scissors
- pencil
- tissue paper
- wrapping ribbon
- foil
- glue
- sponge
- clear food wrap

1  Tear strips of tissue paper and glue onto a card background.

2  Draw outlines of fish, crabs and starfish on card. Paint and cut out. Stick on background.

Stick on pieces of clear food wrap for a watery effect

3  Make coral shapes from card and sponge. Paint and stick on the sea scene.

4 Make seaweed by sticking strands of foil, ribbon and tissue paper onto the picture.

5  Draw outlines of seahorses on dark paper, cut out the silhouettes and stick onto the picture.

Down, down, down

What lies beneath the ocean waves? People have always wondered what mysteries lie in the dark depths. Over the centuries, many different ways of exploring the oceans have been tried. Divers are continually discovering more of the secrets of the world's oceans.

SPONGE DIVING

The earliest form of diving involved divers simply holding their breath for a long time underwater. Early sponge divers in the Mediterranean would dive off a boat to a depth of 30 metres.

As soon as their breath ran out they had to come back up to the surface. In the mid-19th century, divers started wearing heavy diving suits with an air supply to the helmet. This allowed them to go t a depth of 70 metres. However, diving to greater depths created a new problem – the 'bends'. If divers come back up to the surface too quickly, the nitrogen in their air supply forms bubbles in their blood and this can lead to paralysis or death. It was only in the 1960s that divers found a way of dealing with the bends. Today sponge divers wear lightweight suits and breathe filtered air.

WHAT IS SCUBA?

SCUBA stands for 'Self-Contained Underwater Breathing Apparatus'. It was invented in 1943 by Jacques Cousteau and Emile Gagnan. Divers breathe air from oxygen tanks fitted onto their backs. This allows them to move around freely while they are underwater. Scientists can scuba dive to study the oceans, marine life and to salvage wrecks. Lots of people simply scuba dive for enjoyment, and to explore reefs and take underwater pictures.

Deep-sea diver

WHAT YOU NEED

sand

glue

muslin

paste

clay

yoghurt pot

black material

pencil

cocktail sticks

paints and brush

scissors

newspaper

1 Soften the clay and make a head, boots and gloves. Leave to dry. Paint.

2 Cut 2 body shapes out of the muslin and glue together, leaving a hole at the top. Pour sand in and glue the hole closed.

3 Glue the head, boots and gloves onto the sand-filled body.

5 Put the muslin body into the black suit and glue together.

Make a belt from a strip of paper. Stick on 2 small brick-shaped pieces of clay as shown. Glue this around your diver's waist.

4 Draw 2 bigger body outlines on the black material. Cut out and cover both with PVA glue to make the material stiff. Leave to dry.

6 Cut the yoghurt pot into a helmet shape. Paste on strips of newspaper. Leave to dry and paint. Make a grid from cocktail sticks to fit across the front of the helmet.

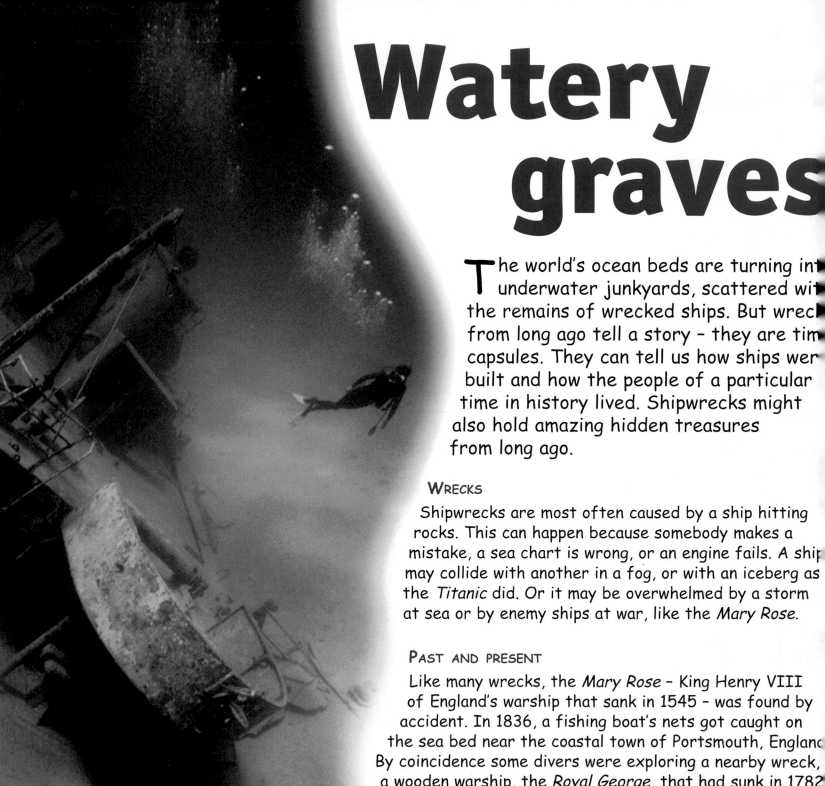

Watery graves

The world's ocean beds are turning int[o] underwater junkyards, scattered wit[h] the remains of wrecked ships. But wrec[ks] from long ago tell a story – they are tim[e] capsules. They can tell us how ships wer[e] built and how the people of a particular time in history lived. Shipwrecks might also hold amazing hidden treasures from long ago.

WRECKS

Shipwrecks are most often caused by a ship hitting rocks. This can happen because somebody makes a mistake, a sea chart is wrong, or an engine fails. A ship may collide with another in a fog, or with an iceberg as the *Titanic* did. Or it may be overwhelmed by a storm at sea or by enemy ships at war, like the *Mary Rose*.

PAST AND PRESENT

Like many wrecks, the *Mary Rose* – King Henry VIII of England's warship that sank in 1545 – was found by accident. In 1836, a fishing boat's nets got caught on the sea bed near the coastal town of Portsmouth, Englan[d]. By coincidence some divers were exploring a nearby wreck, a wooden warship, the *Royal George*, that had sunk in 1782. They also recovered bronze cannon and iron guns from the *Mary Rose*, but it was only in the 1970s that moder[n] technology enabled the wreck and its treasures to be brought ashore. Before this was done, plans of the ship were drawn, photographs taken and all of the 17,000 objects found were recorded.

Shipwreck!

Oceans

WHAT YOU NEED

...rted ...dboard ...es

small pebbles

sand

egg boxes

pencil

...ured ...ard

glue

sequins

paint and brush

...sue ...per

...ors

1 Paste glue over a piece of card and cover with sand.

2 Glue together boxes, card and cartons to form a shipwreck. Cut out jagged edges for a hole in the ship. Paint.

3 Cover half of the base with blue tissue paper to form the sea. Use scrunched-up paper and eggbox cups for rocks, and paint.

4 Make a treasure chest from a small carton. Add sequins for treasure.

What other objects might have washed up on shore?

5 Glue the shipwreck and treasure chest onto the sand and sea base.

Glossary and Index

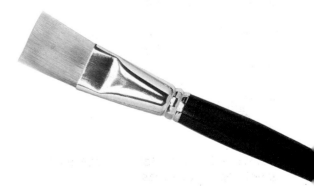